Introduction to Artisan Perfumery

Angie Andriot

Alyssa Middleton

Introduction to Artisan Perfumery
By Angie Andriot and Alyssa Middleton

ISBN-13: 978-0615802268
ISBN-10: 0615802265

Copyright © 2013 by Alyssa Middleton
Cover Design by Angie Andriot
Printed in the United States of America
Published by Beauty For Ashes Press

DEDICATION

This book is dedicated to all the makers of the world.

TABLE OF CONTENTS

1 HISTORY OF PERFUMERY

Ah, the joys of mixing fragrances! When done right, perfume is more than a mere olfactory experience. It is a travel through time, a mythical adventure, an artistic masterpiece, and a (mad) scientist's creation. In the end, perfume is about people. It's our connection to culture, tradition, history, mythology, spirituality, and by extension, each other. Mixing fragrances requires a dash of artistry, a splash of imagination, and a healthy dose of mad scientist. Embed this activity in the centuries-old craft of perfumery, and you have more than just a nice-smelling ointment; you have a little piece of creation made by your own hands. Plus, you have connected yourself to a rich and vast tradition of harnessing the power of scent.

The art of perfumery is over 4,000 years old, with roots tracing to Mesopotamia, Egypt and China. Although nowadays we think of perfume as a sublimely scented liquid we can apply to our skin, the word itself originated with the French, who coined the term "parfum" to describe the fragrant smoke obtained from burning aromatic substances. In fact, "perfume" comes from the Latin phrase *per fumare,* or "through smoke." This early form of incense marks the first historical appearance of perfume.

Perfume originated as a deeply symbolic and often spiritual act. Frankincense, myrrh, and other aromatic woods and resins, were often burned as a part of religious rites. In fact, some cultures originally reserved the rights to burn incense as solely for the priesthood and higher officials. In Egypt, it wasn't until the Golden Age that perfume was released to the masses; before that it was only used in rituals honoring the gods and pharaohs. The early Catholic Church had similar rules about the burning of certain incenses, viewing such an act a sacrament.

It wasn't long before people realized that these fragrances also did a nice job of covering foul odors, which were plentiful back in the days before indoor plumbing and regular bathing. The next stage in the evolution of perfumery was to use fragrances not to cover one's own scent, but to block the scents of others. In fact, upper class folks would wear specially scented gloves when venturing into town so as to inhale the scent of the glove instead of those around them. From this practice grew scented handkerchiefs, necklaces and lockets, and eventually perfume.

2 PERFUME INGREDIENTS

Perfume can be made in a variety of ways. In this section, we cover the most common ingredients used in the creation of perfume. We examine their strengths, weaknesses, and usefulness. Most simply, perfume is comprised of a fragrance and a base-the ingredient to which the fragrance is added. This is often referred to as the "carrier" because it carries the scent. A carrier is necessary because many fragrances are far too pungent and are sometimes even unsafe for direct skin contact. The carrier performs a triple function: dilute the scent, extend the fragrance, and protect the skin. The most common carriers are *alcohol*, oil and wax.

The second component of the perfume is the fragrance itself. A fragrance can come from natural sources such as essential oils and *absolutes*, or from synthetic sources such as fragrance oils and aroma chemicals. Some people have strong opinions about the use of natural versus synthetic products in their perfume. Others have strong opinions about what comprises natural to begin with. Here we cover all the ingredients, as well as the pros and cons, and leave it up to the reader to decide.

Aroma Chemicals

Most perfumes on the market today are made from a combination of natural and synthetic ingredients. The most basic form of ingredient is the *aroma chemical*. These are essentially, chemicals with smells, manufactured in a chemist's lab, either through extraction, *distillation*, or synthesis.

The modern perfume chemist uses aroma materials from two main sources: crude oil, and isolates of essential oils. These can be *nature identical,* meaning the same chemical compounds can be found in nature, or they can be invented by humans.

Fragrance Oils

Fragrance oils are typically a combination of synthetic and natural substances. They can be distinguished from *perfume oils,* in that they are not diluted in an oil base. What we call fragrance "oils" and essential "oils" are often not oils at all, but rather a substance that simply has properties similar to oil. As such, one way to test whether the fragrance oils you have purchased are actually perfume oils is to try to mix them with alcohol. Since oil and alcohol don't mix, then you have a simple way to test whether your "oils" have actual oil in them.

With fragrance oils you can achieve scents that cannot be extracted naturally, such as Lily of the Valley, or replicate scents that are often too expensive, such as Rose. Because they are made synthetically, fragrance oils also tend to cost quite a bit less than *essential oils* and have fewer rules regarding proper storage and protection. However, fragrance oils will vary in cost according to the price of the ingredients used to make them. Also, as with so many other things, the price is often a reflection of the quality.

It would take reams of paper to list all the fragrance oils that are commonly used in perfumery (really—your imagination is the limit!), but here is a brief list of some of our favorites, including the type of *note* and *fragrance family* (described in greater detail later in the book):

Table 1: Fragrance Oils by Note and Family		
Fragrance Oil	**Note**	**Family**
Almond	Top	Gourmand (edible)
Amaretto	Heart	Gourmand (edible)
Amber	Heart	Gourmand (edible)
Apple	Top	Fruitaceous (fruity)
Apricot	Heart	Fruitaceous (fruity)
Chocolate	Base	Gourmand (edible)
Cinnamon	Heart	Gourmand (edible)
Coffee	Base	Gourmand (edible)
Fig	Heart	Fruitaceous (fruity)
Frankincense	Base	Arboraceous (woody)
Fresh Cut Grass	Heart	Verdant (green)
Fresh Dirt	Base	Terrestrial (earthy)
Fresh Water	Top	Verdant (green)
Green Tea	Top	Verdant (green)
Honeysuckle	Heart	Efflorescent (floral)
Jasmine	Heart	Efflorescent (floral)
Lavender	Heart	Efflorescent (floral)
Leather	Base	Terrestrial (earthy)
Lilac	Top	Efflorescent (floral)
Maple	Heart	Arboraceous (woody)
Musk	Heart	Terrestrial (earthy)
Myrrh	Base	Arboraceous (woody)
Oakmoss	Heart	Terrestrial (earthy)
Orange Blossom	Top	Efflorescent (floral)
Rose	Heart	Efflorescent (floral)
Rosewood	Heart	Arboraceous (woody)
Sage	Heart	Verdant (green)
Strawberry	Heart	Fruitaceous (fruity)
Tobacco	Base	Terrestrial (earthy)
Vanilla	Base	Gourmand (edible)
Vetiver	Base	Terrestrial (earthy)
Watermelon	Top	Fruitaceous (fruity)

All Natural Fragrance Oils

An all-natural fragrance oil is one that is made entirely from natural isolates and essential oils. So what is a natural isolate? Here is the definition from the Natural Perfumer's Guild:

> *A natural isolate is a molecule removed/isolated from a natural fragrance material, as defined by the Guild, which contains the isolate. Processes that are acceptable for removing/isolation are: fractional distillations, rectifications and molecular distillations of natural fragrance materials as defined by the Guild*

There has been a lot of debate recently on these natural isolates. It all boils down to how the isolate is made, and what it is made from. One reason a lot of people steer clear of fragrance oils is because so many fragrance oils are made from petrochemicals, then diluted. Natural fragrance oils, however, are NOT. Natural fragrance oils are blends of isolates that are derived through many of the exact same processes that are used to get essential oils – namely, *distillation*. The difference is in whether you are extracting an entire *compound* (essential oil) or a single molecule (natural isolate).

The isolate is more pure - how much purer can you get than a single molecule? However, what it gains in purity, it loses in completeness. You would NOT use fragrance oils - even natural ones - for *aromatherapy*, because they do not retain the entire essence of the original plant material. You CAN use them for aromachology (the psychology of aromas), however, because that is all about the psychological effects of the scents, not the medicinal ones.

Natural fragrance oils provide an excellent middle ground for those looking for something all natural, but cannot afford the high prices of essential oils. For example, whereas a quality rose absolute will run you around $150 per ounce, an all-natural rose-scented blend will cost around $10.

Essential Oils

Essential oils are concentrated liquids taken directly from the roots, bark, leaves, stems, flowers, or other part of a plant. Most essential oils are distilled from a plant using steam or water. The oil carries a distinctive scent (also called "essence") of the plant. Essential oils are used in aromatherapy, which is a centuries-old practice of using natural essences to promote mental and physical well-being. Essential oils vary in price, and are typically more expensive than fragrance oils, but well worth the additional cost for the aroma and psychological benefits they bring to the field of perfumery.

Take the time to research essential oils and learn how each can be used; for instance, lavender essential oil is used to calm and relax and promote deeper sleep. Sandalwood essential oil is considered to be very sensual and often used in fragrance formulas designed to increase attraction and arousal. Because essential oils are so concentrated, they should not be placed directly onto the skin, nor taken internally; doing so can cause serious health complications. Some essential oils, particularly those of citrus fruits can cause photosensitivity, which makes the skin very sensitive to sunlight. While the amounts of essential oils used in perfumes are very small, still pay attention to where the perfume is applied (if using a solid perfume), as that area may become more reactive when in the sunlight.

Some essential oils should not be used during pregnancy or with other health conditions. The following are some essential oils that are hazardous and should NEVER be used:

Bitter Almond	Cassia
Mugwort	Pennyroyal
Rue	Sassafras
Wintergreen	Wormwood

The following pages contain a chart of some essential oils commonly used in perfumery and their benefits.

Table 2: Essential Oils by Note and Benefit		
Essential Oil	**Note**	**Benefits**
Bay (Laurus nobilis)	Heart	Primarily considered a masculine scent. Has reviving, clearing and antiseptic properties.
Benzoin (Styrax benzoin)	Base	Comforting and protecting while elevating mood. Sweet fragrance that is comforting to those who are grieving.
Bergamot (Citrus aurantium bergamia)	Top	Bright, sunny scent often used to aid depression and anxiety.
Black Pepper (Piper nigrum)	Heart	Highly stimulant oil that is warming and has slightly aphrodisiac qualities.
Cedarwood (Cedrus atlantica)	Base	Familiar masculine scent that is fortifying and calming. Helps to instill confidence and reduce fear.
Chamomile, German (Matricaria chamomilla, Matricaria recutita)	Heart	Soothing, calming and balancing. Calms nerves and soothes anxiety.
Clary Sage (Salvia sclarea)	Top	Highly euphoric scent often used to ease depression, anxiety and stress.
Clove (Eugenia caryophyllata)	Base	Restoring and stimulating oil that has strong pain-relieving and antiseptic properties.
Coriander (Coriandrum sativum)	Top	A gentle oil from the spice family, it is reviving and used to stimulate creativity and boost energy.
Cypress (Cupressus sempervirens)	Heart	Warming, soothing and grounding scent traditionally used in purifying incense. Instills wisdom and strength.
Frankincense (Boswellia carterii)	Base	Deeply calming and revitalizing, used as offerings since ancient times.
Geranium (Pelargonium gravolens)	Heart	Helps balance out moods. Similar to rose. Has antiseptic and antidepressant properties. Creates a sense of security and comfort.
Ginger (Zingiber officinalis)	Base	Warming and stimulating, often used to physically and psychologically warm the body and emotions.
Grapefruit (Citrus paradisi)	Top	Bright, refreshing scent alleviates stress, tension and depression.
Helichrysum (Helichrysum italicum)	Base	Cleansing, calming, healing and grounding, often used to lift depression and lethargy.
Jasmine (Jasminum grandiflorum)	Base	Called 'Queen of the Night' since the flower is most fragrant at night. Floral, exotic notes inspire euphoria and is an often used aphrodisiac.
Lavender (Lavandula angustifolia, Lavandula officinalis)	Heart	Soothing, calming and balancing to skin and moods. Helps promote restful sleep. Has antidepressant and sedative properties.

Essential Oil	Note	Benefits
Lemon (Citrus limon)	Top	Bright citrus scent great for revitalizing the mindset.
Lemongrass (Cymbopogon citratus)	Top	Refreshing, uplifting and stimulating oil with strong antiseptic and deodorant properties.
Mandarin (Citrus reticulata)	Top	Has slightly hypnotic qualities which promote restful sleep. Overall is soothing and cheering.
Melissa (Melissa officinalis)	Heart	Called 'The Elixir of Life', a revitalizing, uplifting scent.
Myrrh (Commiphora myrrha)	Base	Long history of healing, used in first aid since ancient times. Inspires peace and tranquility.
Neroli (Citrus aurantium)	Top	Also called orange blossom. Calming, soothing and uplifting. Beneficial in relieving anxiety and stress.
Orange (Citrus sinensis)	Top	Called the "Smiley oil" for its joyful, familiar scent.
Palmarosa (Cymbopogon martinii)	Heart	Delicate floral scent used in skin care for its skin revitalizing properties. Good in perfume to relieve stress and restlessness.
Patchouli (Pogostemon patchouli)	Base	Known as the 'hippy' oil, used extensively in perfume as it adds a sensuous, exotic, erotic note to blends.
Peppermint (Mentha piperita)	Top	Refreshing and cleansing, with antiseptic and astringent properties. A bold scent that promotes clarity and alertness.
Petitgrain (Citrus aurantium)	Top	Very popular in eau de cologne. Recommended for nervous tension and anxiety. Clears troubled emotions.
Rose Otto (Rosa centifolia, Rosa damascena)	Base	Relieves anxiety and sadness. Soothing and uplifting aroma. Has antidepressant and sedative properties.
Sandalwood (Santalum album)	Base	Gentle, erotic scent that appeals well to both men and women. Strong aphrodisiac properties.
Vanilla (Vanilla planifolia)	Base	Soothing and comforting.
Vetiver (Vetiveria zizanoides)	Base	The 'Oil of Tranquility' helps in centering and grounding. Earthy scent popular with both men and women. Deeply relaxing scent.
Ylang Ylang (Cananga odorata)	Base	Soothing, euphoric and erotic scent often used to treat anxiety and release inhibitions.

Essential oils can sometimes be expensive or difficult to find. You can substitute some less expensive oils in your formula with similar, though not exact results. Below is a list of common substitutions for essential oils.

Essential Oil	Substitute Oil(s)
Lemon	Lime
Peppermint	Spearmint
Mandarin	Sweet Orange
Sandalwood	Equal parts Benzoin + Cedarwood
Rose	Geranium
Neroli	Ylang Ylang
Jasmine	Ylang Ylang
Melissa	Equal parts Petitgrain + Lemon
Vanilla Absolute	Benzoin
Patchouli	Vetiver
Tangerine	Orange
Cypress	Cedarwood
Clary Sage	Equal parts Sage + Nutmeg
Clove	Cinnamon

Absolutes

While most essential oils are created through steam distillation or cold pressing, absolutes are created via *solvent* extraction. One of the first challenges faced by early perfumers was that some organic products are just too delicate for steam distilling. An excellent example of this is Jasmine. In order to extract the scent from Jasmine, one must use less harsh techniques, coaxing out the fragrance slowly.

The most traditional version of this method of extraction is *enfleurage*. In enfleurage, the blossoms are laid out in a tray of fat. The fat will slowly draw out the scent as the petals die. This process is repeated until the fat is saturated. If it remains as is, it is called a "pomade." If, however, we then incorporate alcohol, the fragrance molecules will move into it and out of the fat. Once the fat separates out, it gives up its scent to the alcohol. Then the alcohol is allowed to evaporate off. We are thus left with the fragrance "absolute."

However, enfleurage is a time-consuming method that has been eclipsed by modern science. Nowadays we can use solvents to extract the fragrant particles, then distill this down to a waxy solid called a *concrete*. This concrete is then treated as the fat from days of old: ethyl alcohol is mixed in, then separated out and evaporated off--leaving behind the precious absolute.

Because the process of solvent extraction is more delicate, absolutes often carry scents that are "truer" to the original plant, than do essential oils. They will often smell fresher than essential oils, and are favored over essential oils by many natural perfumers.

However, it is also common for absolutes to carry traces of the solvent used to extract them—the extent of the scent will vary by quality of the absolute. As such, aromatherapists tend to prefer essential oils, and it is especially imperative that perfumers find good quality absolutes to work with.

CO2 Extracts

CO_2 extracts bridge the gap between the gaseous distillation of essential oils and the liquid extraction process of creating absolutes. In CO_2 extraction, we take carbon dioxide—something that is typically a gas—and we liquefy it. Well, sort of. We turn it into a supercritical fluid (and no, that doesn't mean one that is always telling you what's wrong with you). Supercritical carbon dioxide is basically a fluid that holds some properties of gas (like expanding to fill a container) and some properties of liquid (like being dense enough to pour).

This supercritical fluid is gaining popularity as a solvent. Chemists can use supercritical CO_2 to extract the fragrant essence of the organic material, similar to the method used to make absolutes. As such, CO_2 extracts have some of the same benefits as absolutes:

• They can extract scent from more delicate substances

• Because the plant material is not being subject to extreme heat, the resulting fragrance is more true to its source. In fact, CO_2 extracts are often closer to the original than are absolutes—and without the introduction of potentially toxic or harmful (or smelly) solvents.

We breathe carbon dioxide all the time; it's perfectly safe. This makes CO_2 extracts suitable for aromatherapy, whereas absolutes are not. Although CO_2 extraction is a relatively new field of science, it is quite promising! With CO_2 extracts, it is possible to bridge the gap between perfumery and aromatherapy while still maintaining high quality natural fragrances.

3 CARRIERS

A perfume is made of more than just fragrance. Once the fragrance formula has been devised, the raw materials are added to a *carrier*—a base material that "carries" the scent. The carrier has three functions:

Protect the wearer. Many essential oils and fragrance oils are potentially harmful when applied directly to the skin. They can be slightly caustic, contain allergens, affect the way the sunlight interacts with our skin, be irritating, cause rashes, etc. Additionally, essential oils often have effects on the body based on the nature of the plant from which they were derived. While some effects are positive, like the healing power of lavender, even good things can be bad in large doses. Diluting the oils in a carrier can reduce these problems.

However, before using any oil as a key ingredient in your perfumes, we strongly advise you research the specific properties of the oils and then test them in small patches on your skin.

Lift and carry the scent. The base you use will influence the length of time a perfume lasts and the range at which others can smell it. For example, an alcohol base will carry the scent further because the alcohol evaporates off and takes some of the fragrance with it. On the other hand, an oil base will keep the scent close to your skin because the oil soaks into your pores.

Dilute the fragrance. Many fragrance ingredients are quite pungent on their own; the scent is often too strong to wear without a carrier—even if the fragrance ingredients are safe—and many of us would prefer not to rudely announce our presence with a thick cloud of fragrance trailing in our wake. What we seek is a subtle enhancement to our general aroma, and that requires toning down the fragrance we wear with a diluent as a base.

In this section, we cover three of the most common categories of fragrance bases: alcohol, oil and wax. We explore the benefits and properties of each, the most common choices among perfumers, and the process of making perfume with each base. Additionally, we look at some other common perfume additives, like preservatives and antioxidants.

Alcohol

The most common carrier for perfume is alcohol—and by this we don't mean that you can run out to the nearest liquor store, pick up a fifth, add some fragrance, and call it a perfume. While common liquor can work to an extent, it is certainly not ideal for making high quality perfume because the actual amount of alcohol in most liquors is rather slim.

Have you ever noticed that liquor bottles always come with a number on their label that refers to its "proof"? An alcohol's proof refers to how much actual alcohol is in the liquor. For example, a high quality vodka might be about 80 proof. To determine the percent of alcohol, divide the proof by two—that's just 40 percent alcohol by volume.

In order to fully dissolve the compounds of a fragrance, you need good, pure ethyl alcohol. Higher alcohol content means higher clarity: without it, your perfume becomes grainy, sludgy, and unexciting.

So what's the solution? Many small-scale perfumers and hobbyists turn to a product aptly called Everclear. This liquor is 190 proof—that's right, it's about 95 percent pure ethyl alcohol. There's all kinds of warnings on the bottle about drinking this stuff straight. Basically, don't. It's great for making perfume, however, and as its name implies, it will provide the "clarity" of scent you desire.

Now, some will say ethyl alcohol is also a good carrier because it does not have a scent of its own. Others strongly insist alcohol does have a scent. Either way, when you make a perfume with alcohol, the carrier is the first to evaporate away. After a few seconds, all that is left behind is the fragrance itself.

Another option for alcohol-based perfume is something called *perfumer's alcohol.* This is basically ethyl alcohol that has been denatured (i.e., someone added something to it to make it undrinkable). Perfumer's alcohol will also sometimes have other ingredients, like an emulsifier (something that helps oils and alcohol blend together happily) or an emollient (thickening agent), or a fixative (fragrance extender).

A note of caution: Alcohol is flammable, and the purer the alcohol, the more flammable it is. This is where the term "proof" comes from. Back in the day, before fancy scientific tools could determine the alcohol by volume, one would sprinkle the liquor with gunpowder and then set it on fire. The color of the flames would be an indicator of how much alcohol was in the liquor. Yellow flames indicated low alcohol content. Blue flames were ideal, and would appear when there was at least 68 percent alcohol by volume. These blue flames were "proof" of the alcohol's strength.

Another note of caution for people considering going into the perfume business: There are some rules you should bone up on regarding shipping and selling alcohol-based perfume. For example, current USPS regulations prohibit the shipment of perfume via any method but ground (so no Express Mail, no Priority Mail). And although current federal regulations (26 U.S.C. 5002, 5171) do not prohibit the sale of perfume made with alcohol you already paid sales tax on by buying the liquor at a liquor store or grocery store, you should check with your state to find out what their specific rules are.

Oils

Any number of oil combinations can be used when making perfume. The most commonly used oils are jojoba, fractionated coconut, and sunflower oil. However, you can create unique products by substituting another oil into your formula. Below is a chart explaining different properties and benefits of specific oils typically used in the making of perfume.

Table 3: Carrier Oils by Benefits	
Oil (Latin Name)	**Benefits**
***Almond, Sweet (Prunus amygdalus dulcis)**	Non-greasy oil that spreads easily and absorbs well. Good for sensitive, itchy or irritated skin. Softens and conditions.
Apricot Kernel (Prunus armeniaca)	Light, silky oil that absorbs quickly. Good for all skin types, especially sensitive, dry, and/or maturing skin. Has a short shelf life, refrigerate after opening.
Avocado (Persea gratissima)	Large amounts of vitamins A, D & E, protein and amino acids make this heavy oil great for dry, sun damaged skin, eczema and psoriasis. Penetrates easily and helps regenerate skin.
Castor (Ricinus communis)	Very thick, sticky oil that contains a unique and beneficial mixture of triglycerides or fatty acids. Castor creates a soothing, protective barrier on the skin.
Coconut (Cocos nucifera)	Solid at room temperature, but melts on skin contact. Its strong antiviral and antibacterial qualities are good for healing wounds and dry, itchy skin. Will not clog pores and absorbs easily. Indefinite shelf life.
Fractionated Coconut (Caprylic / Capric Triglyceride)	This is coconut oil that has been modified so that it remains liquid at room temperature. The liquid is clear and remarkably thin – its molecules are even small enough to fit through the holes in many atomizers. It leaves a less greasy residue than most oils, and has an indefinite shelf life.
Cranberry Seed (Vaccinium macrocarpon)	Easily penetrates skin, and is highly moisturizing. Its high level of Vitamin A means it is good for acne/blemished skin. Provides relief of itchy, scaly, irritated skin. Has a long shelf life. Used to help extend the shelf life of other oils.
Flaxseed (Linum usitatissimum)	Often used to aid with eczema, psoriasis, rosacea, acne and aging skin. Can soften and heal skin abrasions and improve the overall health of skin. Keep refrigerated, and add extra antioxidants to your formula as this has a very short shelf life.
Grapeseed (Vitis vinifera)	Very light oil good for acne and oily skin. Absorbs well without feeling greasy. Mildly astringent to tighten and tone the skin. Has a short shelf life.

Oil (Latin Name)	Benefits
*Hazelnut (Corylus avellana)	Light, strong smelling oil best for oily/combination skin. Easily absorbed and slightly astringent. Keeps best in fridge and has a short shelf life.
Hemp Seed (Cannabis sativa)	Called "Nature's perfectly balanced oil", hemp is high in vitamins A, E, protein, and essential fatty acids. It is easily absorbed and highly moisturizing to leave skin soft and smooth. Has a short shelf life, keep refrigerated.
Jojoba (Simmondsia chinesis)	Not oil, but a liquid wax very similar to our own sebum (skin's natural oil secretion). Great for acne or oily skin, as sebum dissolves in jojoba. Rich in Vitamin E, it absorbs quickly and helps skin retain moisture. Indefinite shelf life.
Meadowfoam Seed (Limnanthes alba)	Said to moisturize skin and hair better than most oils. May also help to extend scents in products. Has naturally occurring antioxidants and a long shelf life.
Olive (Olea eurpoaea)	Moisturizing and mild, olive oil is good for dry, sensitive or baby skin. It is a heavy oil with humectant properties, so it attracts and holds moisture in the skin. Helps soothe itching or inflamed skin. Penetrates deep into the skin.
Peach Kernel (Prunus persica)	Light, penetrating oil good for all skin types. Absorbs easily and leaves a slight greasy feeling. Excellent for facial massage, and is a good makeup remover. Use this oil for blemished or scarred skin.
Rice Bran (Oryza sativa)	Very high in fatty acids. Natural antioxidant. Moisturizing, mild oil good for mature, delicate , dry or sensitive skin.
**Soybean (Soya hispida)	Light, inexpensive oil that is easily absorbed.
Sunflower (Helianthus annuus)	Inexpensive, easily absorbed oil, good for all skin types. Leaves a slightly oily feeling. Helps skin hold in moisture and manufacture new cells. Use high oleic sunflower oil, as it is naturally more stable and resistant to rancidity.
Watermelon (Citrullus vulgaris)	Light, non-greasy oil that moisturizes extremely well, doesn't clog pores or prevent the body from naturally eliminating toxins through the skin. Helps to restore elasticity. Has a long shelf life and is very expensive.
***Wheat Germ (Triticum vulgare)	Thick, slightly sticky oil with a distinct smell. Has very high antioxidant properties, and is often added to other oils to extend the shelf life. Great for aging skin, scars and stretch marks. Penetrates deep into skin and helps repair sun damage. Dilute with other oils.

*Do not use if you have nut allergies.
**Do not use if you have soy allergies.
***Do not use if you have wheat or gluten allergies.

Beeswax

Beeswax is blended with oils and fragrance to create solid perfume. Beeswax can be found in natural chunks or in refined pastille (pellet) form. It is either a shade of yellow or bleached white (either by sun or chemicals). We recommend using refined beeswax for your solid perfume, as this ingredient has been purified of any residue from being in the honeycomb. It is your choice as to whether you want to use yellow or white beeswax. It will not affect the end result of your solid perfume, other than the color.

Antioxidants

As you can see from the chart of oils on previous pages, some oils have short shelf lives and can go rancid (spoil) quickly. Adding antioxidants to your formula can help protect against rancidity. Antioxidants are very different from preservatives, and the two should not be confused. Antioxidants help to protect oil from spoiling, whereas preservatives protect against the growth of bacteria, mold, and fungus. Two commonly used antioxidants are Vitamin E and Rosemary Oleoresin Extract (ROE). Vitamin E (Tocopherol) is thick and easily blends with other oils. Rosemary Oleoresin Extract is a very thick, dark, natural extract that takes a little longer to blend with other oils, but works very well. ROE has an herbal scent that is often unnoticeable in the final product. Some oils are thought to extend the shelf life of other more fragile oils, so you may want to consider using some of the following oils in your formulas: Jojoba, Meadowfoam and Wheat Germ. The formulas in this book do not require preservatives, so they are not discussed here.

Other Ingredients

Also found in many perfumes are various ingredients meant to extend the life of fragrances, help lift and carry the most volatile top notes, combat the drying effects of alcohol, and help keep the components from separating out. These ingredients can be naturally or synthetically derived. However, as the formulas in this book do not involve such additives, we do not discuss them here.

4 FOUNDATIONS OF PERFUMERY

In order to make perfume well, it is useful to know some of the foundations and traditions of fragrance design. This section covers three main topics: fragrance families, notes, and basic blends.

Fragrance Families

Fragrance oils and perfumes are typically categorized into a set of fragrance families. These are simply ways to group the scents according to their various similar attributes. There are many industry standards for how these categories are organized. After studying these category systems, we have taken the best of each and combined them into the following fragrance family guide.

> *Efflorescent (Floral):* Evoking true floral scents, efflorescent oils represent a slightly feminine and highly traditional component of the perfumer's table. Floral essences include Rose, Jasmine, Lavender and Honeysuckle, adding charm to nearly any scent.

> *Fruitaceous (Fruity):* These scents bring the cool freshness of fruit to the perfumery. This category includes fruits of numerous types and origins, and can be further subdivided into fruity and citrus. Examples include Bergamot, Apple, Strawberry, Fig, and Watermelon. Each provides a touch of subtle sweetness to the perfumer's formulations.

> *Gourmand (Edible):* We call the scents that bring to mind the lusty passion of fragrant edibles "Gourmand." These oils bring deep, heady notes to a fragrance—as decadent as the foods from which their scents derive. Examples include Vanilla, Amaretto, and Chocolate.

> *Arboraceous (Woody):* These scents bring forth the character of woods and resins. Arboraceous scents represent some of the most historic and storied scents available to the perfumer, including Myrrh, Amber and Cedarwood.

> *Verdant (Green):* Composed of lush, green scents that call forth the fresh vegetation of spring and summer, verdants are a breath of

renewal in almost any fragrance. Included in this category are Green Leaf, Fresh Cut Grass, Green Tea, and Fresh Water.

Terrestrial (Earthy): For the deep, alluring scent of nature's rebirth, one must look to the earth below. Terrestrial scents do just this, evoking the subtle tones found in fields and forest floors. This category can further be subdivided into earthy and animalistic. Terrestrial scents include Tobacco, Fresh Dirt, and Oakmoss.

Notes

Fragrance oils are classified by their "notes" or scent characteristics. Following are the typical classifications that are used in classifying scents:

Top Notes: These normally evaporate very fast. They tend to be light, fresh and uplifting in nature and are usually inexpensive. Top notes are highly volatile, fast acting, and give the first impression of the blend. However, they are not very long lasting.

Heart Notes: These give body to the blend and have a balancing effect. The aromas of heart notes are not always immediately evident and may take a couple of minutes to establish their scent. They are normally warm and soft fragrances.

Base Notes: These are very heavy fragrances. The scent will be present for a long time and slows down the evaporation of the other oils. These fragrances are normally intense and invigorating. They are normally rich and relaxing in nature and are typically the most expensive of all oils.

Blending Fragrances

Although it is possible to make single-note perfumes (i.e., perfumes with only one scent), it is much more common to mix different scents together. In fact, that's the fun part! But where to begin? Well, oils in the same category generally blend well together. And it's also good to try to get at least one top note to lift the scent, one base note to ground it, and one heart note to bridge the two—beyond that, follow your nose! But to get you started, below are some categories that generally blend well together:

- Florals blend well with spicy, citrusy and woodsy oils.
- Woodsy oils generally blend well with all categories.
- Spicy and oriental oils blend well with florals, oriental and citrus oils. Be careful not to overpower the blend with the spicy or oriental oils.
- Minty oils blend well with citrus, woodsy, herbaceous and earthy oils.

You can also try out the following base recipes and see how they work for you!

Sample Fragrance Blends

Vibrant: A fresh, crisp scent – great for summer		
Drops	**Scent**	**Note**
12	Apple	Top
10	Green Leaf	Top
7	Cedarwood	Heart
1	Amber	Base

Second-Hand Lioness: A sultry, rich fragrance		
Drops	**Scent**	**Note**
12	Jasmine	Heart
5	Lavender	Heart
3	Fig	Base

Parlor: A rich, smoky fragrance		
Drops	**Scent**	**Note**
10	Fresh Cut Grass	Heart
12	Jasmine	Heart
3	Tobacco	Base

Midnight Stroll: An uplifting mysterious fragrance		
Drops	**Scent**	**Note**
23	Cassie	Top
8	Bergamot	Top
1	Ginger	Heart
12	Amber	Base
2	Sandalwood	Base

Spring Dew: A light floral		
Drops	**Scent**	**Note**
13	Lilac	Top
10	Tea Rose	Top
1	Tuberose	Heart
1	Tonka Bean	Heart

Fairy Berry: A fruity sweet scent		
Drops	**Scent**	**Note**
7	Raspberry	Top
4	Fresh Water	Top
3	Blueberry	Heart
1	Vanilla	Base

Sample Essential Oil Blends

Still Waters: A calming blend		
Drops	**Scent**	**Note**
10	Ylang Ylang	Base
12	Sweet Orange	Top
12	Petitgrain	Top

Fairy Wings: A delicate scent		
Drops	**Scent**	**Note**
5	Mandarin	Top
5	Petitgrain	Top
10	Lavender	Heart
5	Ylang Ylang	Base

Earth Goddess: An earthy, warm fragrance		
Drops	**Scent**	**Note**
10	Ylang Ylang	Base
8	Ginger	Base
6	Patchouli	Base
6	Geranium	Heart

Inspire: An uplifting, floral blend		
Drops	**Scent**	**Note**
15	Ylang Ylang	Base
10	Bergamot	Top
5	Petitgrain	Top

Deep Forest: A woodsy/floral/citrus unisex blend		
Drops	**Scent**	**Note**
5	Geranium	Heart
5	Cypress	Heart
4	Bergamot	Top
3	Neroli	Top
2	Lavender	Heart
2	Black Pepper	Heart

Excalibur: A masculine, musky scent		
Drops	**Scent**	**Note**
16	Sandalwood	Base
12	Vetiver	Base
4	Mandarin	Top
4	Petitgrain	Top

Orange Pagoda: A rich, exotic blend		
Drops	**Scent**	**Note**
8	Patchouli	Base
4	Mandarin	Top
4	Petitgrain	Top
4	Rose	Base
4	Sweet Orange	Top
4	Vanilla	Base

5 LIQUID PERFUMES

This is by far the most popular and well-known form of perfume. It is perfume in liquid form. Liquid perfumes generally fall into two categories: alcohol-based and oil-based. There are also special industry terms to denote the dilution ratio of the perfume, and the intended gender of the wearer. However, these terms are about as standardized as are women's clothing sizes. The entire classification system is further muddied by alternate usages of some terms.

For example, in modern language, people often view the only difference between *perfume* and *cologne* as being gender-based. Specifically, if women wear it, we call it a perfume, and if men wear it, we call it cologne. Perfumes also tend to be more floral and more potent, whereas colognes tend to be muskier and less potent. However, traditionally the different types of liquid fragrances are distinguished mainly by their dilution (although even these dilution rates vary by perfume house).

Here is a list that is fairly representative, and has the added clarity of no overlap in percentages:

Splash and Body Spray
These are the lightest products, containing about 1-3 percent aromatic compounds (i.e., fragrance oils, essential oils, absolutes, CO_2 extracts, etc). Typically, it is called a splash when marketed to men, and a body spray when marketed to women. Also, as the names imply, splashes are often sold in bottles without any atomizer attachment, so the men can dab on the fragrance, whereas body sprays are sold in spray bottles.

Eau de Cologne
Contain 4–6 percent aromatic compounds. The term is also often used to distinguish men's fragrances and is traditionally made with citrus oils.

Eau de Toilette
7-10 percent aromatic compounds. The term does not actually refer to toilets, and as such, the literal translation "toilet water" is a tad misleading. A better translation of *toilette* would be "outfit." Eau de Toilettes were originally used on gloves and handkerchiefs, not as something applied to the skin.

Eau de Parfum
10-20 percent aromatic compounds. More common among women's fragrances, but increasingly seen in men's fragrances as well—especially those marketed to young, single men seeking to attract women.

Perfume Extrait

20-40 percent aromatic compounds. You don't see these often, except from artisan perfumers, who are more interested in maintaining the utmost quality than in making the cheapest perfume possible. But don't be fooled into thinking lower dilution always equals higher quality—some scents are better as splashes, and sometimes we only need a hint of fragrance.

Making Liquid Based Perfumes

Mixing perfumes is part art, part science. Although it is helpful to be familiar with the scent families, the fragrance notes, and how these interact, it is certainly not necessary. What is necessary is a creative drive and an adventurous spirit.

Start by testing each fragrance on a fragrance strip. Be sure to label the strip. You can then combine fragrances by fanning the collection of fragrance strips under your nose, adding and removing scent strips until you get the combination you desire.

When you are ready to blend, start with the base notes, as they are strongest. Then add heart notes, and finally top notes. Start with a few drops of scent at a time, and keep track of the number of drops! Write down your recipes, so you can recreate them later. Once the entire mixture is complete, dilute to your preferred ratio with your base of alcohol or oil and pour into your perfume bottle.

The next step is to step back and wait. Close the cap on the perfume bottle, shake vigorously, and then put your perfume in a dark dry place for at least a week—preferably six weeks. The scent will change as time goes on. Impatient? You really should wait at least one day before going back to the scent. This will give both your nose and the fragrance a bit of time to recover.

Here are some tips for getting started:

- When creating a new blend, use the fragrance strips to test out the scent blends. Put a drop of oil on each (labeled!) strip, then wave the strips under your nose like a fan to see how they work together.

- Start off your blending experiments by creating blends that are made up in the following ratio: 30 percent top notes, 50 percent heart notes, and 20 percent base notes.

- Use only the fragrance oils to start. After you have designed the blend, then you can dilute it by adding jojoba oils. If you hate the blend you created, you have then not wasted any jojoba.

- After creating your blend, allow it to sit for a few days before deciding if you love or hate it. The constituents (natural chemicals) contained within the oils will get cozy with each other and the aroma can change, usually rounding out a bit.

- Try sniffing coffee beans between scents to clear out your nose.

- Finally, just have fun! Perfumery has no hard and fast rules. Mix what you think works. After all, it's YOUR nose you have to please!

Equipment/Products Needed

To make a liquid based perfume, there are a few key tools and supplies that you should have nearby:

- Your fragrance materials
- Your liquid base (alcohol or oil)
- Droppers or pipettes
- A graduated cylinder or a scale
- A bottle for your final blend
- Coffee beans (for clearing out the nose)
- Paper towels
- Isopropyl alcohol (for cleaning up spills)
- A pen and paper for recording your formula

Before You Start

Be sure to use clean, dry equipment and utensils. If you are making perfumes to sell to customers, be sure you are following Good Manufacturing Practices (GMP), which include among other things, sterilization and proper workplace preparation. For more information on Good Manufacturing Practices, visit the United States Food and Drug Administration's website:
http://www.fda.gov/Cosmetics/GuidanceComplianceRegulatoryInformation/Good ManufacturingPracticeGMPGuidelinesInspectionChecklist/default.htm

Liquid Perfume Formula

You will need:

- 1 ml base note (such as amber)
- 3 ml heart note (such as fig)
- 2 ml top note (such as bergamot)
- 24 ml perfumer's alcohol
- 3 pipettes
- perfumer's funnel
- graduated cylinder
- 30 ml perfume bottle

Steps:

1. Lay out all your ingredients so that the fragrances are ordered from bases to top notes, followed by the alcohol. Place a pipette in front of each bottle, and uncap the bottles. Place the caps behind the bottle. This organization helps to keep you from forgetting where you are in the process, or cross-contaminating your ingredients.

2. Starting with the base oil and working your way up, measure out each ingredient into the graduated cylinder by using a separate and dedicated pipette for each oil. If you are using a 10ml graduated cylinder, all the oils will combine to fill to 6 ml. So, fill the base note up to the 1ml mark, the heart note up to the 4 ml mark (1 + 3), and the top note up to the 6 ml mark (1 + 3 + 2).

3. Pour the final blend into your perfume bottle. Cap the bottle and shake. At this step, you will ideally step away from the fragrance, and allow the scents to meld for at least a week. The components will develop and change as they blend.

4. When you return to the fragrance at least a week later, uncap the bottle and insert the tester strip. Sniff. Adjust fragrance as needed, by adding drops directly into the perfume bottle. Record these drops, so you can change the formula and recreate it later.

5. Measure out 20 ml of alcohol using the graduated cylinder. If you are using a 10ml graduated cylinder, this means filling it up twice.

6. Pour the alcohol into the perfume bottle, cap and shake. You now have your first perfume! Ideally, at this point you will walk away from the fragrance, and let it sit for at least a week. This allows the fragrances to meld properly.

To Use:
Apply to *pulse points*. To extend the fragrance, apply to clean skin that has been prepped with a moisturizer. The drier your skin, the shorter the life of the fragrance you apply to it.

Variations:
Altering the base. You can make perfume with pure ethyl alcohol (or Everclear), with any of the oil bases discussed earlier in the book (we recommend jojoba oil or fractionated coconut oil), or with perfumer's alcohol. Each base will influence the smell of the final product a bit, too, so feel free to experiment.

Altering the consistency. We have given you a recipe for a fragrance with a 20 percent dilution—an eau de extrait. If you would like to try the other dilutions, simply alter the ratio of fragrance to base. Here are some basic concentrations, and the required amount of base, for 30ml of perfume:

Type of Fragrance	Concentration Amount	Total Aromatic Compounds (ml)	Alcohol or Oil Fragrance Base (ml)
Splash/body spray	.03	1.0	29.0
Eau de cologne	.05	1.5	28.5
Eau de toilette	.10	3.0	27.0
Eau de parfum	.15	4.5	25.5
Eau de extrait	.20	6.0	24.0

A Sample Formula at Different Dilutions

Okay, say you want to make a perfume. Perfume formulas are typically given as percentages. We have used drops in this book, because when you're just starting, that is the easiest way to work. When you're mixing by the drop, the percentages are taken care of. However, once you are ready to step up, you will need to invest in a graduated cylinder or a jewelry scale. A graduated cylinder will measure by volume (how much space the oils take up), and a jewelry scale will measure by weight (how heavy the oils are). Either is acceptable, just be consistent. Proportions by drop, volume, and weight will be different, because some oils are denser than others. So in the following example, I'll assume you are weighing your oils by the gram.

First, you'd set your container on the scale and hit the "tare" button. What this does is set the weight to zero, even with the container on it. This is good, as the container itself is not part of the weight of the perfume. Let's take a look at a recipe:

Spring Dew: A light floral		
Drops	**Scent**	**Note**
13	Lilac	Top
10	Tea Rose	Top
1	Tuberose	Heart
1	Tonka Bean	Heart

Say I want to translate this into grams. All I need to do is change the word 'drops' to grams, and I'm done. But this formula is just for the scent compounds, undiluted. And perfume is diluted to different degrees, depending on what you want: eau de toilette, eau de parfum, etc. How do you do that? Take the total number of drops. Here it is 25. If I want a eau de extrait, for example, I would then divide 25 by .2. In this case, I get 125. That is the TOTAL amount of perfume. So I would then subtract the 25 from that: 100. Now I know my combination: 100 units of base + 25 units of fragrance blend = 125 total units.

Here's a chart showing the possibilities. In this chart, I kept the same base amount of fragrance: 25 units (be it drops, milliliters, or grams). This way, all I need to do is figure out how much alcohol or oil base I need to add to the aromatic compounds. Basically, take Column 1, divide that number by Column 2, which will give me the amount of total perfume (Column 3). I then take Column 3, and subtract the number in Column 1. That gives me the amount of alcohol or oil base to add to my aromatic compound. Make your perfume by mixing Column 1 with Column 4! Here it is again in steps:

1. Divide Column 1 by Column 2
2. Put the answer in Column 3
3. Subtract Column 3 from Column 1
   Put the answer in Column 4

Type of Fragrance	Total Aromatic Compounds	Concentration Amount	Total Perfume	Alcohol or Oil Fragrance Base (ml)
Splash/body spray	25	.03	833.33	808.33
Eau de cologne	25	.05	500	475
Eau de toilette	25	.10	250	225
Eau de parfum	25	.15	166,66	141.66
Eau de extrait	25	.20	125	100

Here is a blank chart. It contains the numbers that never change: concentration amounts. But heck, you can even change those if you want – say you find that a .4 concentration is much more up your alley. Go ahead! There are not hard and fast rules.

Type of Fragrance	Total Aromatic Compounds	Concentration Amount	Total Perfume	Alcohol or Oil Fragrance Base (ml)
Splash/body spray		.03		
Eau de cologne		.05		
Eau de toilette		.10		
Eau de parfum		.15		
Eau de extrait		.20		

Now you try. Here is a formula. How much base do you need to add to each formula in order to get at all the different dilutions?

Flower Pot: A floral blend		
Drops	**Scent**	**Note**
7	Fresh Dirt	Heart
5	Jasmine	Heart
5	Rose	Heart
5	Honeysuckle	Heart
2	Vanilla	Base
	Total Aromatic Compounds (Put in Column 1)	

6 SOLID PERFUMES

Solid perfumes are just that: perfume in solid form, rather than liquid based. To use solid perfumes, you just rub your finger against the mixture. Your body heat will make the solid perfume melt slightly. You then apply the liquefied perfume on your finger to your body. Solid perfumes are becoming increasingly popular because they are easy to make, can be packaged in compact containers and are easily transported. No more worrying about the lid of a liquid perfume coming off in your purse and leaking! Solid perfumes also do not contain alcohol, so for those wanting to avoid this ingredient or those whom have difficulties finding perfumer's alcohol, solid perfume is a great alternative.

The biggest drawback to using solid perfume is the tendency for the solid perfume to melt in a warm environment. Solid perfumes should not be left in pants pockets, warm cars or direct sunlight, as the mixture will melt and become a runny mess, often leaking outside of its container. Of course, when the product cools it will solidify again, but in the meantime it may have ruined whatever material it came into contact with (Ask us how we know!).

Equipment/Products Needed

- *Scale* – one that will measure in ounces
- *Bowls* - glass or stainless steel are best (do not use plastic or metal) – for measuring ingredients
- *Spoons/Spatulas* – to scoop ingredients into bowls and for mixing
- *Pyrex-type glass measuring cup* – to melt, mix and pour your perfume
- *Double Boiler*
- *Containers with lids* – to store your finished products

This next formula is written by weight, not volume, so you'll need to "tare" your scale to make sure measurements are accurate. Remember:

- Place the empty container that you plan to measure the ingredient in (i.e., a bowl) on the scale.

- Press "on" or "tare." The scale will set to zero.

- Put the ingredient into the bowl and the scale will measure the weight of just the ingredient and not the extra weight of the bowl.

Solid Perfume Formula

You will need:
- 1 oz fractionated coconut oil
- 1 oz beeswax
- .05 oz Vitamin E (optional)
- ½ tsp (2.5 ml) scent blend

Steps:

1. Measure oil and beeswax into clean, sterilized glass measuring cup and melt in a double boiler over low heat.

2. When fully melted, remove from double boiler and stir to mix well.

3. After the mixture has cooled for a couple of minutes and before the mixture begins to solidify, add the Vitamin E and scent blend and stir to mix well. If the mixture has started to solidify, re-melt over low heat in the double boiler before adding the Vitamin E and scent.

4. Pour into containers and let cool at room temperature until solidified.

To Use:

Swipe finger across solid perfume. Your body heat will cause the perfume on your finger to liquefy. Apply to pulse points and enjoy.

Variations:

Vegan: It is easy to make a vegan solid perfume (one that doesn't use beeswax, which is an animal by-product). Simply replace the beeswax with candelilla or carnauba wax. Since both of these vegetable waxes have approximately twice the stiffness level of beeswax, only use ½ the amount of beeswax that is called for in the formula. For instance, the above formula calls for 1 oz of beeswax, so you'd use .5 oz of candelilla wax instead.

Altering Consistency: If you prefer a different consistency for your solid perfume, add a little more liquid oil if you want a softer base. If the solid perfume is too soft, add a small amount of wax. Simply re-melt the mixture and add either more oil or wax. Once it solidifies, re-evaluate the consistency and see if any further changes are necessary. Take detailed notes so that next time you make solid perfume you'll know exactly the ratio of oil to wax to use to make it exactly right for you!

7 GLOSSARY

Absolute: Also called "essence," this is the material that has been solvent extracted from a plant or flower.

Alcohol: Used in the perfume industry as a solvent. Most commonly used alcohol is ethyl alcohol.

Arboraceous: One of the six fragrance families. Includes woody and resinous scents such as cedarwood, myrrh, and amber.

Aroma Chemicals: Chemical compounds that have a distinct scent. They are manufactured aromas, taken from bits and pieces of various raw materials.

Aromatherapy: The practice of using essential oils to promote physical and mental well-being and treat a variety of ailments, including anxiety, grief and insomnia.

Base Notes: The rich, heavy notes of the perfume that last the longest time. Base notes are also called "fixatives"—they hold the perfume together, making the fleeting top notes last longer.

Bouquet: A mixture of floral notes.

Cloying: A scent that is overly sweet and clinging, which becomes unpleasant as the perfume's note doesn't change over time.

Cologne: A city in Germany where the first version of modern perfumes was made.

Compound: A concentrated perfume mixture before it is diluted or used in products.

Concrete: The mixture of oil, waxes and color that is obtained after an aromatic raw material such as flower petals are extracted with a highly volatile solvent, such as hexane. The term refers to the fact that after the solvent is removed, the mass is solid and waxy.

Distillation: Process of using steam to extract essential oils from a raw material.

Eau de Cologne: A solution of an approximately 3 percent perfume compound in an alcohol or water base. Eau de Cologne is much lighter than a concentrated perfume.

Eau de Parfum (EDP): A solution containing 10-15 percent perfume compound in an alcohol base.

Eau de Toilette (EDT): A solution containing 3-8 percent perfume compound in an alcohol or water base.

Efflorescent: One of the six fragrance families. Includes floral scents such as rose, jasmine and honeysuckle.

Essential Oils: Essential oils are the highly concentrated essences extracted from various plant parts through expression, distillation or extraction.

Fragrance Blotters: Narrow strips of absorbent paper used to smell scent samples. Used to test the evaporation rate of perfumes. Also called testing strips.

Fragrance Oils: Blends of aroma chemicals and essential oils that can be mixed with both oil and alcohol in order to make perfumes.

Fruitaceous: One of the six fragrance families. Includes fruity and citrus scents such as watermelon, apple, and lime.

Gourmand: One of the six fragrance families. Includes dessert and nutty scents such as chocolate, vanilla and almond.

Heart/Middle Notes: The middle phase of a perfume's fragrance evaporation, occurring after the top note fades away. Mainly produced by floral, spicy or woody components and represents the heart of the perfume.

Nature Identical: a molecular compound that has been made in a lab, but is also found in nature

Perfume: From the Latin phrase "per fumare," meaning "through the smoke"—in reference to resins, etc.—burned as incense offerings in ancient times.

Perfume Oils: These are highly diluted, ready-to-wear fragrances with an oil base. They can be distinguished from fragrance oils in that fragrance oils have not been diluted in an oil base.

Pulse Points: Areas of the body where blood vessels are closest to the skin, which gives off more body heat. Primary pulse points used to apply perfume include the inside of the wrists, behind the ears, the bend in the arm, the base of the throat, behind the knees and on the ankles.

Solvents: Liquids used in perfumery for the dilution of perfume oils. The most commonly used solvent is ethyl alcohol.

Terrestrial: One of the six fragrance families. Includes earthy and animal scents such as dirt, vetiver, and musk.

Top Note: The first scent smelled in a perfume. Top notes are light and fresh, and evaporate quickly.

Verdant: One of the six fragrance families. Includes green and fresh scents such as grass, water, and basil.

8 RESOURCE DIRECTORY

Below are companies we recommend when buying ingredients and supplies. While many supply companies are out there, only stores we have shopped with, and had a positive experience with, are listed.

Vetiver Aromatics
www.vetiveraromatics.com
1912 DePauw Ave
New Albany, IN 47150
(812) 518-2173

Brambleberry Soap Making Supplies
www.brambleberry.com
2138 Humboldt Street
Bellingham, WA 98225
(877) 627-7883

Camden Grey Essential Oils Inc
www.camdengrey.com
3579 NW 82nd Avenue
Doral, FL 33122
(305) 500-9630

Eden Botanicals
www.edenbotanicals.com
343 Keller Street
Petaluma, CA 94952
(855) EDEN-OIL

Essential Wholesale
www.essentialwholesale.com
2211 NW Nicolai Street
Portland, OR 97210
(866) 252-9639

From Nature With Love
Natural Sourcing, LLC
www.fromnaturewithlove.com
341 Christian Street
Oxford, CT 06478
(800) 520-2060

Glenbrook Farms
www.glenbrookfarm.com
1538 Shiloh Road
Campbellsville, KY 42718
(888) 716-7627

Mountain Rose Herbs
www.mountainroseherbs.com
PO Box 50220
Eugene, OR 97405
(800) 879-3337

Nature's Garden
www.naturesgardencandles.com
42109 State Route 18
Wellington, OH 44090
(866) 647-2368

New Directions Aromatics
www.newdirectionsaromatics.com
60 Industrial Parkway, Suite 325
Cheektowaga, NY 14227
(800) 246-7817

Perfumer's Apprentice
shop.perfumersaprentice.com
100 Kennedy Drive, Unit 105
Capitola, CA 95010
(831) 704-7342

Soapers Choice
www.soaperschoice.com
30 E. Oakton Street
Des Plaines, IL 60018
(800) 322-6457, ext. 8930

Soap Making Resource
www.soap-making-resource.com
355 E Liberty St. Suite C
Lancaster, PA 17602
(717) 875-8670

The Original Soap Dish
www.soap-dish.com
PO Box 263
South Whitley, IN 46787
(260) 723-4039

Wholesale Supplies Plus
www.wholesalesuppliesplus.com
10035 Broadview Road
Broadview Heights, OH 44147
(800) 359-0944

ABOUT THE AUTHORS

Your trusted guides in this journey to creating unique aromatic delights are Angie Andriot and Alyssa Middleton. Both are experienced at handcrafting body care products and running successful small businesses. We have included our experiences, tips and tricks in this book to save you time and energy in creating your own formulas.

Angie Andriot is the owner of Vetiver Aromatics. She combines her background in artisan perfumery with her training in education and sociology to help people develop custom perfumes that suit their specific fragrance personality. She has been handcrafting fragrances for five years, and has owned Vetiver Aromatics since June 2011.

To connect with Angie:
Website: vetiveraromatics.com
Facebook: www.facebook.com/vetiveraromatics
Twitter: twitter.com/vetiveraromatic

Alyssa Middleton is the owner of Vintage Body Spa and the Bath and Body Academy. She has been handcrafting bath and body products for 15 years and has owned Vintage Body Spa since 2007. In 2011 she opened the Bath and Body Academy to help current and aspiring beauty business owners build their businesses to rapid profitability.

To connect with Alyssa:
Website: www.bathandbodyacademy.com
Facebook: www.facebook.com/BathBodyAcademy
Twitter: twitter.com/BathBodyAcademy

Made in the USA
San Bernardino, CA
11 April 2014